TODAY, I FEEL UGLY
OVERCOMING NEGATIVE SELF-IMAGE

BY: CANDACE NADINE BREEN, Ph.D.

"Today, I Feel Ugly: Overcoming Negative Self-Image"

Copyright @ 2019 Awakened Path Books, LLC

All rights reserved.

ISBN: 978-1-7329486-6-2

Cover Photo credit: Aleksei Todosko

No part of this publication may be translated, reproduced or transmitted in any form without prior permission in writing from the author. The author and publisher are not liable for any typographical errors, content mistakes, inaccuracies or omissions related to the information in this book.

DEDICATION

To all those who are beginning or who are already on their healing journey.

To all those who have supported and encouraged me in both my writing and my work in service to others.

TABLE OF CONTENTS

DEDICATION 4

TABLE OF CONTENTS 5

INTRODUCTION 8

PART ONE: THE STORIES 13

CHAPTER ONE: "LOVE AND CHILDHOOD".... 14

CHAPTER TWO: "ALWAYS UGLY" 30

CHAPTER THREE: "YOU DONE GOT FAT!"..... 33

CHAPTER FOUR: "THE HAIR SYNDROME" 44

CHAPTER FIVE: "DATING HURTS" 56

CHAPTER SIX: "NEW FAMILY IN TOWN"....... 65

CHAPTER SEVEN: "BULLYING" 81

CHAPTER EIGHT: "IT'S NOT OKAY" 101

PART TWO: HEALING 127

CHAPTER ONE: "DEFINE" 130

CHAPTER TWO: ACCEPTANCE 139

CHAPTER THREE: "RELEASE" 148

CHAPTER FOUR: "LOVE" 150

CHAPTER FIVE: "GET UP!" 163

CHAPTER SIX: "POSITIVE ENERGY, AFFIRMATIONS AND MANTRAS" 165

CHAPTER SEVEN: "HELP" 180

CHAPTER EIGHT: "MAINTENANCE" 189

REFERENCES 191

OTHER BOOKS BY THE AUTHOR 193

ABOUT THE AUTHOR 194

HOW TO USE THIS BOOK

This book is divided into two sections. The first section brings awareness to the lasting effects of what people say and do on an individual.

The second section of this book informs and guides those who have been affected of the ways they can begin to overcome the negative impact that trauma can have on their lives.

INTRODUCTION

As a child, I was frequently called ugly and made to feel ashamed of myself. My father would often look at me and say, "You have a big butt." I was no older than ten years old. He would say it at the dinner table, and my younger half-brother would laugh while I hid my tears by lowering my face over my plate of food.

Every day, my father would insult me. I was not an overweight child; I was an average child who was entering puberty much sooner than my peers. My parents divorced when I was in the third grade, and my mother surrendered her custody rights over me (her son was the child of her first husband, conceived when she cheated on my father) and told me that she "didn't love me anymore." That didn't help my self-esteem much. I became so depressed that I would just eat in order to comfort myself.

One summer, I ate so much that I couldn't fit into the outfit I had picked out for senior picture day. Luckily, going back to school caused me to lose the weight and be back to the normal average kid weight. But that didn't prevent my father from ridiculing me.

When I was an adult and tried to create a relationship with my mother, she found an opportunity every time I saw her to cause me to feel bad about myself. She would say things like, "Your arms are fat," "Your butt is getting wide," and "Can you fit in that dress with that wide butt?" All of these things sounded ridiculous because I was a tight size 6 with a nice, flat stomach. And because I did kickboxing, I had muscular, strong and sexy legs. Despite reality, all of these comments made me feel so ugly and unloved.

When I began dating as an adult, I dated insecure men who felt better when they berated me. I remember their comments: "Your hair is ugly," "You have fat feet," and "Your voice is annoying." I never seemed to find anyone who would say beautiful things about me. My depression caused me to feel that all I deserved was to be with someone who made me feel awful about myself, and so I was drawn to that kind of men and so-called friends. I completely ignored the nice guys and nice friends who said good things about me because I felt less than them and felt so ugly in their presence.

How many of us have endured negative treatment because of our low self-esteem? How many of us passed on the good road only to walk on the bad and rocky path? Realize that it is not your fault. I hope that in reading this book, you'll be able to locate the root cause of your depression and low self-esteem, and look at it in a new light. Those who make others feel bad about themselves have issues of their own that they project as a way of dealing with their own depression and low self-image.

How do we come out of this pit of depression and despair? It's not easy. When we give others power over our lives by believing in their lies, we hinder our own growth and development. I am sharing my stories to help you understand how we become depressed, and why we don't think highly of ourselves. You can turn this around. You can wake up and know you are beautiful and worthy. You can have and deserve love. All you have to do is to commit to having better days, and better days shall be yours.

Rev. Candace Nadine Breen, Ph.D.

PART ONE: THE STORIES

The following stories are examples of how our self-image can be negatively affected by everyday events and comments that we think we have ignored. Every action in the universe has an equal and opposite reaction and, in the case of our self-image, things are not that much different. What we do and say has an effect on the vibration of the universe, even if we don't realize it.

My hope in sharing these stories with you is that an awareness to sensitivities would be created, and that actions would be taken to affect positive changes in the way we interact with one another.

CHAPTER ONE: "LOVE AND CHILDHOOD"

My childhood sucked. Unfortunately, that's not uncommon. Our most important years, the years that determine how we look at ourselves, begins at home, whatever that home environment may be. All too often, the adults have their own unresolved issues that may stem from their own childhood. In effect, these issues end up being projected onto their children, therefore continuing the cycle.

I remember that when I was a child growing up in my very dysfunctional home, my parents never hugged me. They never told me that they loved me and, because of that, I desperately tried to be "perfect" for them in order to "earn" their love. Needless to say, all of my efforts did not work as we cannot earn the love of someone who brought us into this world. It should be that they have love for us because they created us. We all know that it doesn't always happen this way. There are issues such as rape that cause a child to not be created out of love, and it may even be difficult for the parents of the child to love them if they chose to bring the unborn child into the world.

My mother's relationship with my father was a very difficult one. She ran away from her first husband to be with my father, who was a handsome, violent, womanizing man. He lied to her from the very beginning, telling her about the imaginary properties and cars he had, and a fairy-tale life on his father's land in the very country part of Alabama.

Soon after, she became pregnant with her first child from my father. Then she had a miscarriage, and my father ended up in jail. Supposedly, my father had beat her until the unborn child was killed. She became pregnant again, but with me; and ran away to Rhode Island, where she met up with her first husband, to whom she was still legally married. There was no love in my creation, thus no love was given to me.

While the other children my mother had were showered with brand-new gifts, elaborate birthday parties, and my mother's welcoming arms, I was neglected; given moldy, old and worn gifts; and had no parties, plus my birthdays were always forgotten. This neglect formed the way I felt about myself very early on.

Since I didn't know why my mother treated her other three children better, I assumed with my childlike mind that I didn't deserve anything good. I was a very depressed little girl. I created my own imaginary world in my bedroom where imaginary people actually loved me. I had fancy tea parties where I received imaginary presents. I had picnics where there was always laughter. In the summer, I would turn on my floor fan, drape a bed sheet across it so that it formed ripples, and pretended I was a mermaid with lots of mermaid friends who had an underwater magical kingdom where every day was a day of celebration!

For a very short while, my mother's first husband showed me love. He had mistakenly thought that I was his child. He showered me with love and affection; and I ate it up like chocolate ice cream! He would pretend I was a potato sack and toss me over his shoulder, holding me by the ankles. I would squeal with excitement. I never remember my mother being around when he took time to play with me. Then my father showed up one day on our front porch, ending that fun relationship. From that moment on, there was nothing but violence, anger and chaos.

I was ten years old when my mother told me in her bedroom one morning that she didn't love me anymore. She told me that she was going to give me up for adoption. Oh no! What did I do? Had I not been good? Why was I being sent away?

Everything suddenly became my fault. I blamed myself for my parents' constant arguing. I thought that if I had been good and my mother had loved me, then my parents wouldn't be fighting all of the time. After my parents physically separated a few years after their divorce became final, my father had informed me that he and my mother never wanted me anyway. "You were a mistake," he said to me.

I cried. I was a horrible child. I didn't deserve to live. Depression became my best friend.

My father also told me that I was responsible for their dissolved marriage, and that I was also the reason why he couldn't find himself a new female partner once he became single again. He told me that I was "ugly" and that I had a "big butt". I was a dog in his eyes;

and his repeated molestation, rape and degradation of me showed me that as well.

None of the blame helped my self-esteem. I felt wretched. I felt as though I didn't deserve anything good. I didn't get anything for Christmas after I was sent to live with my father because I didn't deserve anything. I wasn't allowed to have friends over because I didn't deserve to have friends over. I was an awful child, and my father reminded me of that almost daily. I tried so hard to do everything right, but I failed so miserably that my parents regretted creating me.

I carried all of that hurt and guilt with me into my teenage and adult years. It would not be until nearly thirty years later when someone actually showed me what I had been missing in my childhood. In school, I endured the bullying because I knew that I was "no good". Kids picked on me constantly, and my response was to withdraw. I attempted suicide numerous times, and even begged Spirit to remove the very breath from my body as I no longer wanted to be among those of the flesh. I didn't belong here. I didn't want to be here.

Why was I so unlovable? What did I do to make my own parents reject me? What had my half-siblings done that was different? Perhaps, if they weren't so cruel to me, I would have asked my half-siblings what I could do in order to be loved. Everyone hated me. I felt so bad about myself. All I wanted was for someone to love me, to tell me I was beautiful and to hug me. So, with a ruined childhood, I marched into adolescence with a very poor outlook on life.

When children are born into their families, it is the duty of the parents to care for and love that child. It is the duty of the parent(s) to ensure that the child is safe; and has the nutrition they need for them to grow up healthy and strong, contributing to their ability to learn and thrive. When a parent mistreats the child, the parent is only creating bad karma for themselves. They may not receive that bad karma in the current lifetime or density, but it will eventually happen. They may not even be aware that they are receiving this bad karma because of what they had done in a past life.

Since the Universe operates out of love, love is what is expected of all the living creatures residing within it. What we put out into the Universe, we get back amplified. So, if we are mistreating children, the most innocent of all living beings, we can expect to reap our rewards sometime later.

My father was terrified of dying. It could be seen in his once-fiery eyes. He had done so much harm to so many people, often without thinking about what he was doing. He was filled with so much anger, bitterness and hatred for what he himself had endured during his own childhood.

My father was mistreated by his father, sexually abused by his stepmother, and forced to do hard labor on the family farm, thus prohibiting him from going to school. Because of his lack of education (he only had a third-grade education and was, at one point, still in the third grade at thirteen years old), he couldn't read or write well enough to function in the world around him. He was angry because he wanted to learn; but as a Black adult male in the 1940s and 1950s, he didn't know what resources were available to him in order to at least get a high school education. His frustration turned into bitterness, which morphed into anger, then into hatred and then into violence. There were stories of him once killing a man by putting him into an industrial oven at the place he worked. He was once a wanted man in the South, and somehow avoided being captured.

    My father didn't seem to have a conscience when he hurt people. Thinking back on his life, I wonder if he ever wanted to "be bad". Does a person ever really want to be angry and hurt others? If someone had a choice, would they choose to murder and abuse people? I don't think my father really wanted to be the way he was. I think that he hadn't developed the inner strength he needed to prevent the actions of the lower -vibrational energies he had allowed to permeate his soul. With the lower-vibrational entities in his soul, he felt powerful and in control, something he had never felt in his entire life because his own father seemingly took away all of his opportunities, his future and his potential by working him like a dog on the family farm while his own ten brothers and sisters had the chance to go to school.

When my father's health had seriously declined, he became painfully aware that his time was coming to an end; and he was scared. He knew the life he had lived. A week before his death, he had been praying constantly, something he hardly ever did (on the occasions when he did pray, I am not so sure he was praying to the Divine Source because he was so entrenched in dark energies). He was suddenly reading the African Bible he owned (he never read it because he couldn't read); and it was thought that he had asked for the gift of reading before he passed, and it was granted. He often had the power to get what he wanted from some spirit when he asked, but it was not always something good.

Perhaps he made amends before his demise. Perhaps he promised that he would do the work that he needed to do on the other side in order to raise his own vibrational energy. I'll never know what happened during those last days, hours and minutes of his spirit occupying the flesh I had come to know as my father. All I know was that he couldn't hurt anyone else anymore.

CHAPTER TWO: "ALWAYS UGLY"

When I was in middle school, I was horribly ugly or, at least, that was what I had been told. I had bald spots in my head because my parents thought it was a good idea to have my hair repeatedly chemically processed. My hair, which was once long, thick and wavy, fell out in clumps. I had sores on my scalp, with some sores bubbling and oozing into my increasingly thinning hair. I didn't know how to wash my hair, so I ended up with lice. I had to teach myself how to take care of my hair because no one seemed to want to show me anything about self-care. I always had fast-growing hair; and when I started to treat it well, it flourished. But my father would take me to the salon just as my hair was doing well, and have it ruined yet again. It would be a constant struggle until I was nineteen and living on my own.

The kids at school took advantage of my low self-esteem and unattractive image. In eighth grade, I was voted the "ugliest girl in the whole class" in front of the entire school during our class day, called "Feud of the Classes". I felt my face go hot as everyone laughed. I held back my tears. The popular White girls were voted "most beautiful". The only other Black girl in my class was on the "beautiful" list because she was part of the "in crowd". None of the teachers came to my rescue as most of them despised me and my family. The school was a predominately White Catholic school, and we were neither White nor Catholic. I was never accepted nor loved at that school. A classmate of mine even said that I was "nothing but a nigger."

I accepted that I was this Black, ugly, balding thing with a big butt (the girls in my class even said that my butt was "huge") who was so hideous that there was no way I could or would ever fit in. That solidified the thousands of reasons why I could never be loved, not even by my own family.

CHAPTER THREE: "YOU DONE GOT FAT!"

What does it matter whether someone is slender, round, tall, short, round, pudgy or skinny? Isn't being in good health all that really matters? Why do certain people feel the need to point out the change in someone's body aloud, and to the person's face? The revelation is not always done in a friendly manner, either. These comments are often rude and very hurtful. It took me years to understand that I didn't have to take the comments personally. Instead, all I had to do was look at where the comments were coming from. Many times, it was just the person projecting their own feelings about their self-image onto me.

My mother was one of those people who always seemed to have a negative comment up her sleeve when it came to me and the way I looked. When I used to visit her often at her office in my efforts to make her love me, she'd ridicule me in front of her employees (who would lower their heads and pretend they didn't hear her).

During this time, I was exercising and working out a lot, so I had a strong, lean and fit body. One day, when I visited my mother's place of business, I came in wearing a sleeveless top and skirt. She took one look at me and said, "Your shoulders are fat." Instantly, I felt ashamed. I think she was very well aware of my insecurities, and took advantage of that. For many, many years following this remark, I stopped wearing sleeveless tops in public.

Another time, my mother said something about my weight when my boyfriend at the time bought me a cute dress. When I showed it to her, all she said was, "Can you get into it? Your butt is getting wide!" That infuriated me. First of all, my butt was tiny in comparison to hers and a lot of other people I knew. Second of all, I was working out a lot and had a very slender waist that made it difficult to keep my pants up. She could have told me that the dress was beautiful instead of saying something negative. I didn't know why she felt the need to constantly say negative things to me any time I was around.

When I was getting married, I reluctantly invited my mother, incorrectly thinking that she'd change and be proud of me and, hopefully, finally love me. I was dead wrong. Following the wedding, I received a lengthy email from her that tore my heart in two. She had nothing nice to say. She said that I "looked fat" in my wedding dress and that my "legs were fat." She wrote, "You say you've been working out, but your legs are fat." Why all this talk about fatness? I wasn't the least bit fat, and her comments really hurt me.

Shortly after my wedding, my mother had surgery on her stomach that made her pencil-thin. When I saw her in a store, I hid from her. I was pregnant and didn't want her to see me and make horrible remarks. When I saw her from my hiding place in the store, I couldn't believe how horrible she looked.

It was at that moment when I realized that all those negative comments were not about me, but about the way she felt about herself. She was even sporting heels like I used to wear, and her attire looked ridiculous on her. What people choose to wear never bothered me, but remembering all of those hurtful comments she threw my way made me angry. I could feel the fiery anger burning in the pit of my stomach as I watched her trying to keep her balance in the very high platform heels that were my signature attire. She was trying to be me! She was trying to be me because she hated herself. It looked odd on her because it wasn't who she really was. She hadn't accepted or loved herself, so she decided to lash out at me. Then, when no one was looking and after she had successfully pushed me out of her life, she tried to make herself look and dress like me. She even wore makeup, which she never really did!

My oldest half-sister was the same way as my mother. She would talk about my legs. I always had very strong legs because I walked a lot and I rode my bike, too. It wasn't until 2018 that a good friend of mine told me that I had sexy legs, and that made me feel good. I was wearing short shorts because it was just so excruciating hot. I often covered my legs due to my past shame; but this time, I didn't. I needed that confidence boost. My friend also said to me, "You should show those legs more often!" Such a sweet and kind friend!

I stopped mailing out photo cards during the Christmas season because of a comment made by my grandmother. I called her to check and see if she received the card; and she said, "Yes, I got it. You done got fat, though." That hurt me. She didn't say "nice card" or "lovely picture", but something negative. It was then I decided not to send her any more photo cards. I wondered why my family all had such a poor self-image. Perhaps it had nothing at all to do with me.

The hurtful comments didn't end with my grandmother. A comment from my half-aunt caused me to not wear sandals for a few years. She told me one day that my feet looked fat in my sandals. I know I shouldn't have let that bother me, but I hadn't yet built up an impenetrable wall that would prevent me from being hurt. I had a lot more work to do on myself before I became strong and negative comments no longer bothered me.

What did I learn from all of this negativity? Sometimes, people say mean and hurtful things out of jealousy or because of some hurt that they experienced in the past. They project their negative self-image onto others, sometimes unknowingly. Instead of being met with anger or hostility, these people need to receive the healing powers of love. They are hurt and fragile. They need understanding and help. It is not expected that we are the ones who will help them on their journey to healing, but we can just take a moment to step back and see the situation for what it really is: pain.

Unfortunately, pain is a great motivator in this world, and causes people to hide behind false images that they have created in order to inflict their negativity onto others. These people don't always have control over the thoughts that persist in their minds. They have an internal battle going on and may not know they need help. If they are aware of this, they may be too proud or ashamed to reach out and ask for it. With love and understanding, healing can happen for all. But first, we must break down these barriers we've built around ourselves and allow ourselves to be vulnerable enough to be comforted.

CHAPTER FOUR: "THE HAIR SYNDROME"

Hair, hair, hair! Hair can make or break a person, or at least some people believe so. Hair can make an average-looking person glamorous and a glamorous person average. Hair maintenance costs millions of dollars a year worldwide in products, wigs, extensions, styles, dyes and cuts. We spend a LOT of money on trying to make our hair look what society tells us is "nice".

Being born a Black woman didn't make hair matters any less challenging for me. Our people have some serious hair issues. There's "good hair" (I thought all hair was good if it covered your head), kinky hair, "nappy hair" (these two words together irritate me), "curly hair", and "weave". The list goes on and on. What always got to me was that our own people would shame another member of our race for wearing their hair naturally—the way it was when they were born. Slavery has caused us to feel that we were ugly in our naturalness. We were never seen as good enough. Our hair was too tough, our skin too dark and our lips too big. I grew up with all of these negative stereotypes and found that members of my family bought into these concepts of beauty as well.

I was born with a full head of thick, long, and curly dark hair. My mother, who made weekly visits to the salon to have her hair straightened with a hot comb, hated my hair and did her very best to destroy it. Her other children, who were my half-siblings, would tease me and call me "White" because I had a lighter complexion and my hair had a different texture than theirs. I never understood why they saw my being different as negative. My mother doted over her other children's hair, taking her time to wash and style their hair; and would often ignore me. I wasn't old enough to understand how to wash and style my hair on my own, so my hair went undone, often resulting in lice and lifeless hair.

At one point, she convinced me to go shopping with her.

Instead, she took me to a salon, where my hair was processed with chemicals that burned my scalp and made my hair fall out in clumps. For years, I had bald spots, and my mother seemed satisfied that her other children looked better than I did. I was devastated as all the children at school would make fun of me.

After years of trying to get my hair back to as natural of a state as I could and after repeated cuts, I decided to grow dreadlocks. I still have them to this very day. At first, I added hair onto the ends to help with the growth. But when they grew past my waist, I chopped off ninety percent (some of them were too much a part of my natural hair) of the extensions and just let them be. Even then, I received shouts and hostile comments.

One day, I was picking up a take-out meal at Panera Bread. A woman of color who was clearly in a bad mood rolled down the window of her minivan, drove around the block and shouted at me, "That SHIT is fake!" If the comment had been said a few years earlier, I would have taken it personally, but I knew that the problem wasn't me. This woman obviously had issues with herself and was just projecting her negative self-image onto me.

Why does hair have so much power and cause people to become so violently angry? Good question. It is just hair, after all. My grandmother once bragged to me that a relative of hers didn't have "nappy hair". In fact, her words were, "Ain't none of my peoples got nappy hair", as if it were something to be proud of. Where did these negative thoughts originate? One answer: the demonization of our African ancestors mixed with slavery. Black people have not recovered from what slavery has done, and racism didn't and doesn't help at all. We don't even know why we don't like another Black person who happens to come into our sphere.

Years before I became a Spiritualist Minister and Healing Minister, I was a member of an African American urban Baptist church. I loved to sing and was a member of two choirs. I sang alto and was pretty darn good, too. Sadly, there was always so much drama in that church, which really took away any good message that the church tried to spread. Hair hatred was such a major issue. I witnessed women really be cruel to other women because of a preconceived thought that certain women had "better hair" than they did. I mean, there were other issues in the church as well, but for the sake of this book, we are only going to discuss hair.

Looking back on my years at this church, I see that pain and self-hatred were ridiculously apparent and visible. Somewhere in their lives, these people were fed lies about themselves. They would doll themselves up for church every Sunday and strut into the doors looking like a million bucks. But inside, they were just small, insecure people who really needed to be loved, to be healed, and to be told that they were beautiful without all the exterior decor.

I, too, was one of those women. I had the fancy and expensive hats and dresses, perfect makeup and pressed hair; and I walked in my heels as though I were on stilts. It was a fake confidence driven by societal norms that told me that unless I adopted the "right" look everyone else did, I was nothing more than an ugly spot in the way of something society saw as beautiful.

I know that the issues mentioned previously don't just stop with my culture and race. Similar issues can be seen across all racial, ethnic and cultural lines. Who is the "they" who determines what is acceptable and unacceptable in appearance, and why does this "they" hold so much power? Is it to sell products to people they see as easy money targets? Is it to promote their own brand? What messages do we continue to pass down onto our youth when we buy into the idea that we are not good enough just the way we are? Why must we fight among ourselves when one member of our tribe dares to be different or dares to accept and love who they are naturally? Why do we have such a hard time embracing our own uniqueness and three-dimensional beauty? These are tough questions to begin to answer, and we have a long way to go as a society in order for us to fight back against the negative propaganda that weaves and streams its way into our lives.

I wish that one day, my grandmother would be able to love herself before she transitions from her current incarnation. I hope in her next incarnation that she'll be able to see herself as beautiful, no matter what form she takes. She has spent so much of her current lifetime ashamed of the way she looked and adopting a false pride from people who were not her true blood relatives. She used to tell us that we were Native American of the Cherokee tribe, and something in me just didn't believe her.

I had my DNA tested, and her story was shown to be false. She kept saying that her father's wife was Cherokee and was her mother; in fact, the woman wasn't found in my grandmother's ancestral tree to be her mother. I did my own research because I felt that I was being told false stories that had been passed down as truths, and that the only way I'd ever find out who I am was to do my own extensive research. When I discovered my roots, I cried, not because I was sad, but because I finally had an answer. I had no problem accepting my DNA. I could finally say with confidence what I am in terms of my ethnicity, and it felt good. I may not be accepted by others who have similar roots, but I am proud of where I come from. My hope is that those who are currently ashamed will someday embrace their heritage and love themselves as well.

CHAPTER FIVE: "DATING HURTS"

When we choose to get involved with someone, there is always a risk. We put ourselves "out there" and expose ourselves to the pool of flesh-eating sharks who often drown out the gentle dolphins. It can be scary and wonderful all at the same time. As the saying goes, "You'll never know if you don't try."

What we often don't get told is that we should prepare ourselves for encounters with those I like to call the "brick -throwers", people who just want to hurt you because they have some deep-seated anger. It makes them feel good to see someone else hurt. Think of it as a sort of high for them. When we get involved with these types of people, we don't know what baggage they are carrying with them. We only meet their representative and not the real person; the real person comes out much later. I have learned very quickly to spend time being friends with someone before I jumped into a deeper and more intimate relationship with them.

As a young woman, I fantasized about having my Denzel Washington, just like many other women across the globe had been doing ever since Denzel came to the big screen. I thought I had found him in a guy I dated when

I was in my late 20s. He was tall, dark, handsome and educated. He worked in his family's property business. His parents were wonderful and so deeply in love with each other. I loved watching his parents interact; they were adorable. I had never before witnessed parents being so loving toward each other; and so I fell for them hook, line and sinker.

What I didn't know was that their son was a real jerk. He had so many personal issues that he had to project them onto others. His main issue was self-hatred. Even though his mouth didn't actually verbalize his hatred of himself, he said it in so many other ways. He was a beautiful mocha chocolate color. He had gorgeous curls. He was tall and lean. He had gorgeous white teeth. I thought he was beautiful. He thought he was ugly. He did his best to tear me down, not because of his dislike of me, but because of his dislike of himself.

"You have fat feet," he told me one summer when I walked around his apartment barefoot. I was both stunned and ashamed. Looking down at my small feet, I began to think that my feet were, indeed, fat. From that moment on, I made sure to cover my feet at all costs whenever I was around him.

"Black women are ugly," he said to me that same summer.

"Your mother is Black," I reminded him.

"Yeahhhhhh, that's different. She's my mother," he responded, rolling his eyes up toward the sky. I was beginning to tire of his hurtful comments that seemed only to increase during this particular summer when we would part ways. Why was it that we Black women were always being put down as though we had a hand in creating our DNA, as if ANYONE on the planet had a hand in creating their DNA?

"Makes no difference," I spat out.

"It does. I'm not dating my mother." I was beginning to understand what was going on. He continued, "Spanish women are much sexier! They have that beautiful hair and wear those tight clothes—"

"WHAT?!!!" I couldn't take any more insults. I got in my car and drove away. The next thing I heard was that he had been messing around with a Latino woman while he was supposedly dating me. He finally broke up with me in order to be with her. Although I felt burned, I went on with my life. I started dating someone else (who later turned out to be a jerk as well), and then I received a phone call one January morning.

"Happy New Year," the voice said. I instantly knew who it was.

"What do you want?" I said, my voice not revealing my pleasure in his attempt to crawl back to me.

"So, how are things? How are you doing?"

I couldn't believe that he had the nerve to call me and act like we were good old friends catching up with each other. I remained silent. I knew he could feel the chill my silence sent through the phone.

"Look, I am dating someone right now," I said.

"I just wanted to say 'Happy New Year'," he said, sounding defeated.

"Yep, that's great, bye." I hung up the phone without waiting for him to say anything else.

What surprised me was that he called me after he had dumped me a year or so ago. I assumed that things didn't work out with his Latino woman; so he had decided to try to contact me and make up, and then I'd be exposed to the possibility of being hurt all over again. Once a jerk, always a jerk. At least, that's how I saw things. I wasn't about to walk back into a relationship knowing he how he felt about Black people—his people. I would rather be alone than allow myself to endure that abuse again.

He would not be the last jerk I'd date, but I was not going to stick around once I uncovered the truth about anyone I let into my life on a romantic level. I wanted to be loved and accepted for who I was, whether it was seen as good or not-so-good. I wasn't going to settle for anything less. No one culture, color, race or ethnicity should be seen as better than the rest. If a man couldn't see that, then he wasn't worth my time.

CHAPTER SIX: "NEW FAMILY IN TOWN"

When my family and I first moved to West Barrington, Rhode Island, there weren't many biracial families or people of color. There I was with my long dreadlocks, my curly-haired brown children and my White husband—a rarity in our town—and we stood out like a sore thumb. My daughter would often complain that she was the only "brown-skinned" kid in her class, which was true for all of her elementary public school years.

There was another mixed-race family that came along, who were like us except the mother was White, the father was a big and tall African dude with dreadlocks, and the children were a shade or two darker than mine. We bonded almost instantly, yet that didn't end the treatment we received from those unaccustomed to seeing people like us in a town like Barrington.

When my daughter was in preschool, there was an Asian mother who spoke very little English. I quickly figured out that she was desperate to fit in with the Barrington elite and, thus, behaved in a manner that was crude and rude toward anyone my shade. Her son was out of control, and she did nothing about it. In fact, she seemed to encourage it. She allowed him to bully my daughter and, on one occasion, he pushed her down onto the ground, causing her to get a bloody scrape.

At that time, my daughter was taking up karate, and I told her to use the defense techniques to fight back when the boy bothered her again. On a morning when all of the parents were waiting for the school doors to open, I watched the boy grab my daughter from behind. Instantly, she flung her head back in the defense method she was recently taught in class, hitting the boy's face with the back of her head. The boy crumpled to the ground and my little daughter ran to me, tears streaming from her eyes. She wrapped her little arms around me, and I told her that she did a great thing and that I was proud of her for standing up for herself.

I suppose the boy's mother was very upset at my daughter for defending herself because after that day, she turned her attention toward me. Loudly, and in front of me, she would make comments about my dreadlocks. She scored a few giggles from the other parents, yet I kept silent. I didn't want to show my angry side, the side that I had worked so hard to suffocate. Once that can of anger was opened, there was no way I could control it, and I really was afraid of being taken away from my children. So I chose not to react. The woman seemed to think that her only leverage was her comments about my dreadlocks despite the fact that her own hair was falling out and bald patches were scattered about her head. I saw her actions as jealousy, and endured the giggles and audible comments without visibly reacting.

Everywhere I went in town, I stood out like a sore thumb. It took a while before I felt comfortable enough to even go to the town library, to the town post office, or even to the local stores. Initially, people treated me as though I were carrying two loads of smelly garbage into their place of business. It irked me. We owned a house, we paid taxes, and we had just as much right as everyone else to live here. Why were people so rude?

We kept to ourselves in our neighborhood. We had purchased one of the biggest houses with the biggest private backyard in the neighborhood, and that alone was cause for dislike. One neighbor asked me who I was when I was retrieving our trash containers one day. A widowed woman, another neighbor, thought I was my husband's housekeeper; and I had to set her straight.

"He is my husband," I said to the widower, who was standing in my driveway.

"Oh," was her reply. She walked away. How insulting. Was it because of my skin color?

I began to feel very depressed and alone in our new town. I wouldn't have cared if we sold the house and moved. We had worked so hard and saved so much so we could afford to live in a safer community with good public schools. Why did my appearance have to matter? Why was I being treated so badly? My husband was often at work all day and left early in the morning, so no one really saw him.

I never really thought about my skin color until people made me aware of it by the things they said or by the way they treated me. After all, our only visible differences are those related to our color. We are all the same. When we get cut, we all bleed the same color of blood. We have the same inner organs and we walk and function the same, for the most part. We are the same species, so why is there any prejudice? Why do they stare? Why do they whisper? Why do they ridicule? Aren't we all just merely atoms and particles vibrating at a certain speed that creates the illusion of a solid form? One person's aura comes into contact with another person's aura. One person's energy affects another person's energy. So, if you really think about it, why does one person's skin color matter?

    Very briefly, I had a friend in town who had two children who were the same ages as mine. Our kids played together, and we lived within walking distance from them. She had two boys and her boyfriend, the father of the boys, was very polite and friendly to both my family and me. In a town full of strangers, I thought I had found a friend. When we were both home with our infants, we would have lunch together or hang out together. We laughed and shared so many fun moments.

She had revealed to me that she had cheated on her boyfriend and, because of that, he "wasn't ready" to marry her. The way she and her boyfriend met was not very solid, anyway. When they met, she was engaged to someone else. According to her, her fiancé was "mean to her". Thus, she cheated on him with the father of her children. When she was five months pregnant, she confessed her infidelity to her fiancé, and they broke up. They had a house and everything!

We used to go to yoga together one night a week. On one particular night, she told me that there was a woman she knew whose husband she could flirt with. She said to me, "I bet that if I flirted with her husband, he'd cheat on her." Being a married woman myself, I found this offensive and remained silent. Who would say something like that? She was a bartender, and had been a little too flirty with some of the male customers and she'd tell me about it. She told me about how a man went "out back" with her and kissed her neck. I was repulsed, but tried not to let it show. I really wanted a friend and, for some reason, I thought my marriage was safe from her.

My new friend and I began to get closer. We were BFFs, or so I thought. Out of the blue, she told me one day not to call or text her anymore. I didn't ask why. I just said, "Okay." She then said that she didn't want our kids to play together anymore. Did I overstep her boundaries? My mind searched for the possible offenses I may have caused. I remembered when she was really sick one day and was all alone with her kids, I used a coupon I had and purchased a very cheap cardboard coloring castle for her kids, and for mine as well. I figured that it would keep the kids busy on a rainy day. She texted me, "Don't do that again." I was hurt beyond belief. All I wanted to do was help.

She continued to reject me: she snapped at me one day because she was feeling bad about not going to college. I never judged her or behaved in a manner that would be seen as cocky or superior. She shouted at me that she didn't go to college because she didn't have the money. I figured she didn't want to have college debt like I had, and so many of my friends had as well. She then snapped at me for taking a shower and not looking like I just rolled out of bed every morning when I showed up at our kids' school. I was an early riser. Why was that a crime?

It became evident her problems were not with me, but with herself. She had tossed aside our friendship, and I felt so alone all over again.

To make matters worse, my former friend began ignoring me in public. She pretended not to know me. She began dressing up and wearing tons of makeup. I noticed she was hanging out with the local "elites" in town, the women who didn't work and who spent all their time at the spa or gym. She was trying to be one of them; since I wasn't one of them, I was dumped like a hot knife. To further crush me, she began audibly gossiping about me in front of me with her new crew. She and her new friends would look at me and laugh. They'd laugh and look at me with their fake eyelashes, manicured fingers and tiny waists. I tried not to show any emotion, and began wearing sunglasses to hide the tears that were brimming in my eyes. Was bullying someone with whom she had once been friends a prerequisite to being a part of her new crew?

For almost a year, I endured the bullying of my former friend and her new crew. I'd pick up my kids from school and rush to my car, often driving home in total sadness. I'd tell my husband, and he'd suggest that I just remain strong. But he wasn't me and he wasn't a Black woman with long dreadlocks who was a rarity in town. He didn't endure what I did. My former friend's boyfriend would continue to speak to me, as he does to this very day.

When I began to make friends with other parents, my former friend would befriend them and spread gossip about me; and they would eventually distance themselves from me. The next few years were the most painful years for me in town. I felt isolated. I didn't venture out, not even to go for walks. I often wondered what things were being said about me in order to turn everyone against me. I didn't do bad things, so what gossip could she possibly say about me?

It took me a few years to be able to see her and drive by her house without being affected by our broken friendship.

Despite what my former friend had said and done to me, I didn't hate her. I was only filled with sadness, and the understanding didn't come until later. I had to see the situation for what it was: her own feelings of insecurity. I forgave her after I forgave myself for allowing myself to be hurt by her. I filled my heart with love for her and her family so that when I passed by her house on my way to mine, there was no longer any feelings of anger or resentment.

CHAPTER SEVEN: "BULLYING"

Because I had been bullied for nine long years at my parochial school, I believed that I truly was ugly. It didn't help that my father repeatedly abused me and my mother told me that she didn't love me. My self-esteem was in the toilet and there was little chance, at the time, of it ever being reversed.

When someone is bullied, they withdraw. I became sad and depressed. Who was I going to tell? No one at the school wanted anything to do with my family, and even the principal verbalized to me one day that she was "glad that I was leaving." I'd tolerate the bullying until

I was pushed beyond my breaking point, which often resulted in angry outbursts that would flare up and quickly consume anything in its path.

There was an instance during recess when some kids in my class stole my winter mittens. My mittens were blue and they were big, puffy and warm. They were crocheted, and I loved the comfort they gave my hands. When the kids taunted me, I could feel my anger rising. I did nothing to these kids, yet they continued to bother me! All I wanted was to sit in my little favorite corner in the schoolyard and be warmed by the sun. The sun gave me so much comfort. I would spend recess alone in my sunny corner spot, sheltered from the schoolyard drama.

Somehow, during this particular recess, my mittens fell into the hands of some of my classmates; and they decided to have some fun with me. A boy waved my mittens in front of my face. When I reached out to grab them from him, he threw them over my head to another classmate who stood behind me. The classmate threw it back to him, and I felt my body go scalding hot despite the winter air. I wasn't playing their monkey-in-the-middle game. I just wanted my mittens so I could return to my sunny corner and have a few minutes of quiet solitude.

I angrily walked up to the boy, who again threw my mittens to a classmate. I reached down (he was much shorter than I was. In fact, he was the shortest kid in our class) and grabbed him by his throat. With one hand, I squeezed his throat until his face started turning red. Between clenched teeth, I said to him, "Give. Me. Back. My. Mittens." He choked a few times; and all the humor and playfulness drained from his face, only to be replaced by fear. I increased the pressure around his neck until he struggled to speak.

"OK," the boy said, flailing his arms. "Give 'em back to her! Give back her mittens!" With one hand still around the boy's throat, I looked over my shoulder at the classmate whose face had gone pale. I wasn't playing games. I was so angry and tired of the bullying that I could physically hurt anyone who messed with me. Today, they had gone too far.

The other classmate walked up to me slowly, his eyes glued to his choking friend. When the classmate handed me my mittens, I released the boy, who then fell to the ground, clutching his neck and gasping for air. I knew he wouldn't report me because then he'd have to explain his role in the situation. In the chance he did squeal, I didn't care, anyway. Kicking me out of the school would have been a gift. The two boys scattered like roaches, and I made my way to my sunny corner to take in the last minutes of recess undisturbed.

It's interesting how surprised people are when someone who has been constantly bullied does something extreme. My questions are: Why weren't the adults involved? What types of actions were taken to prevent bullying on school property? Is there any protocol? Are teachers trained in bullying awareness? Are there safe and unanimous ways a student can report being bullied? What is the procedure for the punishment of the perpetrators?

My daughter, my oldest child, was bullied in elementary school. It began in kindergarten, when a classmate of hers started spitting in her face every single day. When my daughter informed me of this, I initially told her to report it to her teacher.

A few weeks went by, and my daughter told me that her teacher just kept ignoring her complaints. I emailed the teacher, who said that she "didn't see anything of the sort". I began staying on the playground in the morning with my daughter before the teacher arrived to pick up the class.

One day, a parent asked me why this particular bully was being mean to my daughter after seeing the girl toss my daughter's backpack. Since I hadn't seen the incident, I decided to be more vigilant on the playground.

When the class was lining up, I watched, much to my horror, as the girl turned around in line and spat right at my daughter's face. Every parent saw it. My heart sank as my daughter crumpled to the ground in tears. My temper flared like a fire in a dry forest. I was pissed and restrained myself from slapping the shit out of that girl.

I approached the teacher, who was standing only two feet away from the girl. "Did you see that?!" I screamed at the teacher. "Did you see that the girl just spat in my daughter's face?"

"I didn't see anything," the teacher said to me coolly, looking down her nose at me.

I couldn't take any more ignorance. "That's it! I am going to the principal!"

I marched to the front of the building, rang the buzzer, and went into the principal's office, requesting a copy of the school's bullying policy. The principal at that time was very lazy and also very condescending when meeting with parents. She spent her days flirting with all of the school-department men who worked in the building. I wasn't going to waste my time with her.

She asked me if I had followed the protocol, and I told her that I had documented proof that I tried to inform the teacher and that I had also emailed her (and she never responded). Leaving the school office in a hurry, I drove down to the district school administration office and demanded to see the superintendent immediately. I could not feel anything coursing through my body except outright rage.

The day following my visit to the school administrative offices, the principal was visited by the superintendent. The principal suggested removing my daughter from the classroom, and my husband told her that "In no way should our child be punished for the bad behavior of another student."

The child's father, who happened to be a really nice guy, approached me the next morning outside the school and made his daughter apologize to my daughter. His face showed the horror and embarrassment he felt at what had happened. Years later, I would come to discover that the girl's father really was a nice person who shared my views, and who spoke up for equality and for what was right. His wife, on the other hand, often looked at me with disgust.

When I was approached by the girl's father, he handed my daughter a bouquet of flowers. The girl handed a card to my daughter and shook her hand. My daughter was silent, and I could tell that she wasn't buying this show one bit. When the father asked the girl to shake my hand and apologize, the girl pulled her coat sleeve over her hand and extended her covered arm to me. I understood the meaning behind what the girl was doing, and waved away her insulting gesture. Where was this kid learning to treat people like this, especially people who were not White like her? She obviously had been taught some horrible habits.

The following year, I would encounter the girl numerous times in school. During one lunch when I was my daughter's guest, I spotted the girl watching me as she silently ate her lunch. She was curious, and probably trying to see if I was the bad or inferior thing that she was being told I was. It wasn't long before the girl was giving me compliments whenever I saw her. She'd say things like, "I like your hair/shirt," etc. She even made a poster thanking me for volunteering in the school library.

It annoys me when adults spread hatred to the young. They teach our youth old stories of hate. That is wrong! Children should be allowed to make their own decisions and judgments. We adults should stop trying to brainwash these kids with our negative views. Let them be free and untainted!

Unfortunately, my daughter continued to be bullied. When she was in fourth grade, she attempted suicide. I remember when I got the call from the school counselor. My heart broke into a million pieces! I had been so vigilant about talking to everyone and anyone about the bullying my daughter was experiencing, but the principal at that particular school (which only consisted of fourth and fifth grade) ignored me constantly; and the teachers could only work with what they were given. I had fought the good fight and, each time, I hit brick walls. I even wrote an article about my daughter's experiences in the local patch. Just when the article was gaining supportive comments from others who had experienced similar situations, the article was deleted from their online publications, and I was then banned from the patch. I am still banned, even at the publication of this book.

It was just easier for the town officials to turn a blind eye or shove issues under the rug rather than deal with them. A girl once hanged herself in her backyard because she was being bullied. What happened? Nothing. The town said it were against bullying; but when an actual incident was reported, it did nothing. It couldn't risk anything that would tarnish its golden reputation, and that was unsettling.

Finally, I gave up; and my husband and I decided that the only thing we could afford was the private religious school (and we weren't religious) across our son's school. Luckily, the school was good for her. She made real friends (even though I was still not welcomed or accepted, especially when my daughter tried to make play dates with her friends), she excelled academically, and even made the high honor roll.

Just when I thought the bullying had subsided for a while, it was my son's turn to endure it at his school. Luckily, the new principal was a take-action leader, and my son's bullying experience was very brief. It so happened that I knew the parent of one of the schoolyard bullies. I also knew that the mother, who was from another country, didn't discipline her son; and would watch him behave in a rough manner toward the children who played on the school playground after school. In her mind, it was just "kids being kids"; but I was not going to stand and watch her son hurt other kids, even if the kids were not mine.

Almost in disbelief one afternoon, I watched the schoolyard bully at my son's school tackle a girl to the ground, and then kick her. The girl's mother did nothing! In fact, she was friends with the boy's mother; and their friendship was based on fear of the boy's mother, who managed to successfully throw her weight around at the school. I reported the incident to the principal, and informed her that I would not allow my son to play on the school grounds after school due to the repeated playground bullying. My son was very sad about not being able to play after school, but I explained to him why I made that decision.

My son endured being picked on by the boy and called names. But my son, unlike my daughter, was not one to wait to be told what to do. He kept complaining to the teachers until he was heard. He was a very persistent child, and didn't really care what "mean people" thought of him. In fact, he marched right up to the boy's mother one day, and told her that he didn't play with her son anymore because he was mean and a bully. I was so proud of him. But what about kids like my daughter, who are often hesitant to speak up? Who is going to protect them at school? What is to be done about those who actively bully and harass other kids on school grounds?

Bullying has lasting effects on children, and can often follow them way into adulthood. For a long time, as an adult, I carried the effects of bullying with me, internalizing them and allowing them to depress me. No one was there to help me, not at school and not at home. Despite my vigilance and intense involvement in my children's schools, bullying still happened. There were attempts to silence me, attempts to pretend that it wasn't happening, and for what? For a district reputation? For the protection of the elite parents? Do schools really care about children like they claim they do, or is it all about covering their own asses and gaining money and prestige?

CHAPTER EIGHT: "IT'S NOT OKAY"

I was in my twenties, and I thought I was pretty good-looking. My makeup was flawless every single day. My clothes were crisp and clean. I worked out twice a day to maintain my curvy size-6 figure. My hair was always up to societal standards. My nails were neatly manicured. I was a professional to the extreme. I had worked hard to get to where I was, studied long hours, and sacrificed so much. I was proud. What other people saw was a woman who was beautiful, strong and confident.

I often drew the eyes of my male colleagues and, for a woman who grew up constantly being told she was ugly, the attention amplified my pride in my exterior appearance. On one occasion, a male colleague shouted at me as I walked my seventh-grade class down to the cafeteria for lunch. He was standing in the corridor with another male colleague who, I hadn't discovered until many years later, had taken quite a romantic interest in me. As I walked by them, the former male colleague loudly said, "Miss Cunningham, Miss Cunningham! Look at that, look at that!"

One of my students who heard the comment looked at me with her mouth open in surprise. My face grew hot with embarrassment. Allowing my students to walk ahead of me, I whirled around and told the man who made the comment that I didn't appreciate him shouting inappropriate and suggestive remarks at me.

The man just laughed at me and waved me away, saying, "Oh, turn around and let us watch you walk away!"

The angry, hot fire within me subsided as I realized that I was not going to get him to apologize or stop. The other male colleague who stood next to him said nothing and just lowered his eyes, as if he didn't approve of his friend's actions. I didn't take the comments as flattering because they were hurled at me in such a grotesque manner that I felt as though I were a prostitute standing on the street corner. There were other ways to express or show admiration that I thought were more polite and respectful.

Some people may say that I should have been thankful someone was noticing me, and it should had made me feel attractive. What my colleague did was disrespectful. I was not a piece of meat being displayed for others to pick over. My colleague and his catcalls disgusted me. It made me want to put a bag over my head and hide. I didn't like the sexual advances or sex-laced comments I experienced at my place of work. I didn't appreciate or like the catcalls.

I felt that my brains were not being acknowledged, and that I was more than just a body.

Men sometimes mistakenly think women try to look good in order to attract their attention. When I was a young professional, I didn't get all dolled up every morning to impress any of my male colleagues. My makeup and nice clothes were my shield. All of that glitter and glam covered up my insecurities, my fears, and my pain. Every day, I went home to an empty house, with no one there to hug me or to tell me that they loved me. It hurt to be alone, but I was too afraid of being hurt to allow anyone decent to enter my sphere.

Some of my female co-workers despised me because, on the outside, I appeared as though I had my shit together. They assumed that I was proud and confident. I was in shape, and this infuriated some of these women so much so that they would verbally lash out at me. I recall a cute and petite female co-worker of mine who became angry when a male colleague complimented me. Both individuals were married, and I was still single. The man said that I had really smooth skin (and I did, but I still felt the need to cover it up with foundation). The woman, who was within earshot, snapped, "No, she doesn't! Look closer; she wears a lot of makeup!" This same woman once had lunch with me and I, foolishly thinking she was trying to be my friend, ended up being hurt. She said to me, "I'm not into clothes, hair and makeup!"

I didn't understand why my colleagues seemed to have mixed reactions to my appearance. It was either seductive or irritating, and these conflicting views only caused me to vacillate between feeling beautiful one day to feeling hideous another day. When a person is told something conflicting repeatedly, they end up being a mental mess!

Despite my attire at work, nothing seemed to prevent me from being sexually harassed. For eight years, I was tortured by one particular male colleague with whom I had to work with closely. He had asked me several times, "If I weren't married, do you think you could be with me?" He even told me that he should have waited a year before he got married because then he would have had a chance to meet me. I would repeatedly tell him that there was no way I'd ever be interested in him, married or not; yet that didn't silence his comments or actions.

My harassing male colleague began to get upset when I showed any interest in someone else, and he would seek to ruin it. He even showed up one night at my house after his summer softball practice. I was dressed in my robe and preparing to read in bed when he rang my doorbell. I blocked the foyer so he wouldn't get any ideas. He seemed nervous, sliding his foot from side to side. I can't believe I was stupid enough to answer the door! I think he caught my uneasiness, and said he had softball practice at the field down the street from my house; and asked me if I'd be interested in attending some of their games. I nodded, knowing that I'd never attend. I wasn't the kind of woman who would knowingly mess around with a married man, although I had been burned by lies from men I didn't know were married in the past. Once my colleague left, I relaxed.

When I moved to Riverside, Rhode Island, my male colleague somehow knew my address; and told me one day that he "knew where I had moved to". I didn't give anyone my address, nor did I even have it changed at work. I was trying to protect myself, yet nothing I did ever seemed to work.

As years went by at work, my colleague began to get bolder with his comments. While we were in our hall duty positions one morning before the students crowded the corridors, he asked, "Do you wear thong or panties?" I was shocked into silence.

My colleague also had some prejudice toward African Americans. He was a Puerto

Rican from New York, and he told me that his mother said that all Black women wanted was sex. He told me that before he met his wife, he briefly dated a Black woman. According to him, he was taking her on a date to the movies when she began to make sexual advances toward him. I didn't believe him, nor did I visibly react to his revelation.

When I broke up with a Black guy I was dating, he asked me,

"Did you use a condom when you had sex with the guy you were dating?" What a personal question to ask me! That was none of his business, and I didn't see why he cared. I was so ashamed and embarrassed to be asked that question that I walked away from him. I was too afraid of repercussions to report his behavior, as he was part of the "good ol' boys" who controlled the building.

When reporting on the school's corruption, a news reporter once called the good ol' boys' group as "The Perry Mafia". I had already witnessed the gang in action, and they were ruthless. Not all of the members were as disgusting as the married colleague who harassed me; some were just part of the group by association, and their membership caused them to be "safe" at work. But there were members of the gang who, in my opinion, were just as guilty as the ringleaders because their silence allowed others to be bullied.

Eventually, people get tired of being sexually harassed every day at work. It can only be ignored for only so long. The victim often does want to report the harassment, but they are afraid to do so, just as I was. When I reported the married colleague who continued to say inappropriate things to me, I was totally thrown under the bus. Not only that, I was flattened by the bus!

The woman in charge to whom I reported the harassment was once a teacher, just like I was. In fact, I was hired one hour before she was, and we had once been good friends. When she gained her position of power, she became one of the good ol' boys. So, of course, she wouldn't let my complaint go anywhere. I was the one who had to suffer, and suffer I did.

It became even lonelier at the school for me. I ate lunch in my classroom with the lights off and the door locked. I often had a book I would read. I would relax, putting my feet up on my desk until it was time for me to tackle my next class. I had five classes every single day, totaling 130 students. At times, I had a hundred and forty-five students. After school, I ran the theater program until the funding went haywire.

When I first began my professional teaching career, I was in heaven. I was part of something big, and I had worked so hard to get there. I was respected, or so I thought. Our building had two lunch rooms: one in the basement next to the cafeteria, which was primarily dominated by the popular crew; and one on the second floor that was gentle and dominated by women. For a while, I had lunch with the second-floor crew, but I felt so out of place. I didn't have a spouse, a stable significant other, or children. I didn't have family with whom I would spend the holidays. In essence, I didn't feel that I fit in at all, and it would just make me very sad.

This brought me to the teachers' lunchroom in the basement next to the cafeteria. The jokes there were not always pleasant. There were some uncomfortable jokes about molestation, rape and abuse; and although I felt uncomfortable, I would nervously laugh. They didn't know my secrets— yet. When they did find out, things didn't get any better. When my secrets were exposed via a poetry book I had self-published, some felt guilty about the jokes that they had said. I thought that my story would serve as a wake-up call that they should be careful with the things they say because they could unknowingly hurt someone. Unfortunately, not everyone saw my story that way.

Sometimes, I regret some of the things that I've done when I was a professional teacher. I regret laughing at some of the jokes because what I did was mask my own pain. I was not being truthful to myself. I should have spoken up more when I knew things were wrong. I should have spoken up for myself when someone said something that offended me. I should not have allowed myself to be continually spoken to in an inappropriate way. I should have been more careful with the romantic partners I brought into in my life. I was like a kitten going into a world full of lions.

I had no prior dating experiences. My father forbade me to date anyone while I continued to stay under his roof, which is why I didn't have my first boyfriend until my second year of college.

Being alone in the big, wide world was hard. It left me bruised and broken. I only saw pain in the eyes of the person who looked back at me in my bathroom mirror. I hated the memories the pain resurrected in times of solitude and depression. I felt as though people could see the ugliness of my past hurt when they looked at me. In my mind, my secrets made me ugly.

In order to fill the cavity in my life, I acquired pets and pretended that they were my children. I loved them, and they loved me. My pet children were a moody iguana named Lady, a shy chocolate dunlop bunny named Susie, two madly-in-love parakeets Peak and December, and a crazy and loyal pit bull-husky dog named Princess. When all these pets either died or were given away, I adopted two kittens: narcissistic Ming (a Chocolate Point Siamese) and wild Nala (a gray Calico). These pets were only Band-Aids, and did nothing for the way I felt about myself.

In my mind, I was nothing. I was nothing but a made-up doll sitting on a shelf, waiting for someone to recognize her, to take her down and to love her. It wasn't going to happen anytime soon. In fact, it didn't happen until about ten years later. I struggled to love myself. I soon realized that I had to love myself before someone else could love me. Sometimes, I felt like a phenomenal woman; and at other times, I felt like someone who was thrown out with the trash. Despite the work I did to love myself I continued to struggle daily.

Just when I thought I was strong enough to stand up for myself in the face of abuse, I slipped up. The comment happened so fast that I was caught off-guard and felt dirty afterward. I cried. How could I have let this happen? He was supposed to be a mentor, a person supporting me on my psychic journey; yet his words berated my integrity. He was so disgusting, and the comment seemingly came from nowhere.

I was seriously talking about a project he wanted to work with me on and he, being a much older man, needed me to explain the technological aspects of the project. In my conversation with my supposed mentor, I said, "This work is coming along nicely!" I was totally excited about the project's developments, and wanted to explain his piece of the project to him over the phone.

"I know, I can hear you breathing hard," he said nonchalantly.

I was quiet. It took me a minute to figure out what he meant. He then laughed loudly, and unnecessarily explained the joke to me. I can't even write down the joke because I feel so ashamed of how I allowed this person to expose me to his bodily-function jokes. My mind went blank and, for what seemed like an eternity, I struggled to hold back tears.

That wasn't his only sexual joke during our conversation. Why didn't I just hang up the phone? I wish I knew. Why didn't I stand up for myself? I don't know the answer to that, either. Being a victim doesn't help matters as well.

What pissed me off was that he was well aware of my experiences, and had read my published memoir. One would think that he would be more considerate and gentle with his words. Unfortunately, I think he felt that it was okay to treat me this way, not caring whether or not he hurt me.

Days after the incident with my male mentor-friend, I wondered what made him think that he could say something like that to me. Did I ever tell him that it was okay to say that to me? How could I do a project with someone who says something like that? How could I ever work with someone like that? Now that I am in control of whom I work with, I don't have to tolerate that, and I can cut those people off simply by just not calling them or ignoring their phone calls.

I often think of Bill Cosby and the image that he portrayed onscreen. There are so many men out there like Bill Cosby. They have a public face, and then they have a private face; and sometimes, they don't even think that what they're doing is inappropriate. Most of the time, the woman just goes along with it; but no one sees the pain it is causing her inside. We women sometimes have to think about our jobs, so we just pretend that we are going along with it. We have bills to pay and children to feed, and we can't just let that go. Who knows who will ever hire us, especially when we get old and have children? It becomes challenging for a woman to get a good-paying job.

It's not okay to say sexual comments to women at all. Joking about the female anatomy or bodily fluids is not funny; it's uncomfortable.

There needs to be some type of sensitivity training or sensitivity workshops that people at work can participate in. They need to be within the communities, at churches, at the local YMCA. Perhaps sensitivity training should be a mandatory part of the workplace environment. There are people who get affected by it. Some turn to alcohol and drugs; some turn to suicide. We never know because it's done in silence.

People turn a blind eye to it and, because they do, someone suffers alone.

When will we wake up?

PART TWO: HEALING

After experiencing great trauma, how does a person find their way to healing? I have contemplated this question many times. I wanted to be better than I was. I wanted to think good thoughts about myself. I wanted to see my body as beautiful, and to know that I was just as good as the next person. But that isn't something that can happen overnight, especially when one has been repeatedly battered and abused verbally, mentally, and even physically.

Healing is a journey, not an outcome of a journey. It is the steps that make up the whole healing picture. It is constant, and requires repeated check-ins and maintenance. Your automobile needs gas to run; you also need fuel in order to keep making progress on your healing journey.

The following chapters go into detail about the ways in which we can heal from any type of trauma. I later included these steps in a workshop I have offered to the public called "Ten Powerful Tools for Your Healing Journey". It requires commitment, honesty, and a great deal of reflection. Never begin your journey alone; surround yourself with like-minded and supportive people. Don't put too much pressure on yourself, and always remember why you began the journey in the first place.

CHAPTER ONE: "DEFINE"

This healing journey is all about you, so you need to understand why you are doing this. It is not to please someone else; it is so that YOU can be your best. What are you hoping to overcome? What are you hoping to learn? Are you really positive you want to begin now? If not, when do you want to begin?

Once you begin, you can pause or slow down; but it is important that you make forward movements. It is very important that you don't look at the end result because there is no ending; there is only continuance. No one is ever totally healed and free of any past pains;

we learn how to navigate our lives with the pain that had happened because healing doesn't mean erasing the fact that something negative happened. These unfortunate events help us to grow; expand our consciousness; and teach us more about our lives, the universe, and how to interact with other people so that we maintain a healthy balance in all aspects of our lives (emotional, mental, physical, spiritual, etc.). Healing is not a cure—healing is picking oneself up, admitting that something happened, and learning from it. This learning not only helps ourselves, but also assists us in being able to help others who are at various stages of their journey as well.

Let me tell you, I still sometimes fall back on remembered past hurts. Sometimes, I get into a cloud of depression. It's normal to not always feel our best any time after an incident that traumatized some aspect of our lives. This journey isn't easy, which is why you must decide to at least begin. You may have to begin again and again, but recommit to going forward each time.

I have met many people who have been through unheard-of trauma, and who have even tried to commit suicide. Having been in their place in the past, I was able to comprehend how they were feeling. Even though I knew they really needed to begin their healing journey, I also knew that they couldn't begin until they knew and understood why they wanted to begin. They first had to know that they were going to do it for themselves, and not for anyone else. They were the ones carrying around all the baggage, and nothing anyone else could do would ever change that. Second, they had to ask themselves: Why was it so very important that they do the work involved in their potential healing journey? What would they hope to accomplish along the way (Note: Along the way, not at the end)?

I suggest keeping a journal. This will help you keep yourself accountable to the steps you are taking along your healing journey. You should also go back and read your journal at least once a week.

This is important because there is no sense in doing something mindlessly.

What do you expect to get from your journey? What is the issue or the trauma that needs healing? Why is it important for you to do this? This is the step that often holds people back, and prevents them from healing from their trauma. You need to have a reason to do something, and that reason must not be because of someone else. For example, you shouldn't say, "I'm doing this journey for my kids." No, you are not. Your children have nothing to do with your past trauma. You are doing this for yourself, so the answer has to relate to yourself.

In Alcoholics Anonymous groups, the facilitators tell their members that they they must come to the meetings for themselves, not for anyone else. Alcoholism is a disease, and the people suffering from this disease have come to the group so they can learn how to navigate life and to try to avoid falling into depression and taking up the bad habit yet again. Yes, setbacks do happen, which is why there is such a support group. I like the way Alcoholics Anonymous facilitates their groups, and I know several people who attend group meetings weekly. I like to take this approach when I talk to people about why they are involved in trying to heal from their past trauma. It's the same mindset, in my opinion.

People who are suffering from trauma sometimes take up bad behaviors like alcoholism, drug use, prostitution, overeating, etc. These behaviors are not healthy for them, and they need to stop. Depression, anxiety, and PTSD are all diseases. Therapy helps; but before you even go into any of those situations, you need to know why you are doing it, and you need to know that any behaviors associated with the trauma are not healthy. It is hard to just stop, which is why you need a support group. We will discuss this in a later chapter. For now, we need to concentrate on making the first step to realizing that we need a positive change. We need to really want to commit to changing, and to navigating our lives with this trauma as part of our being.

Just as people in Alcoholics Anonymous groups must live with their disease (although that does not mean they should pick up the habit again), people who are suffering from trauma must also realize that the trauma is not going to disappear; and that it'll always be with us. We must try to live our lives knowing that we have this trauma, but not let it control our lives. We control our lives. This is the message that is used in Alcoholics Anonymous, and it is the message that I like to use in my group workshops as well.

Take control of your life, and realize the negativity is not serving a purpose in your life. Commit to trying to heal and to doing what is necessary in order to live a fulfilling, happy, productive and prosperous life. Once you have that under your belt, you are ready to move on to the second step of your healing journey.

CHAPTER TWO: ACCEPTANCE

We know that we have experienced trauma, and we have to accept that this trauma happened to us. We can't deny that we suffered, and we can't pretend that it didn't happen. So in this next step, we are going to discuss acceptance. This does not mean we are taking the responsibility of the action, as we cannot control how others treat us. But we can say to ourselves, "Okay, this happened to me. I suffered, and now I must move on toward healing." Remember, healing is constant, and you will always be trying to navigate your life with this trauma as part of your being. You cannot erase it, and there is no magic spell or potion that will eliminate it or expel it from your person. You are not judging the action or the person responsible for the action. You are just looking at it objectively. You are acknowledging it; and in acknowledging it, you are working toward constant healing maintenance.

As I mentioned in the previous chapter, I suggest journaling your progress and any thoughts or concerns you may have. I do offer a private Facebook healing group as part of the 10-week class I teach. In the private Facebook group, people are able to talk about their progress, fears, and concerns, as well as any potential setbacks. The private Facebook group is called "Healing Group"; and you can only join it when you take the class as I like to protect people and their privacy, and allow them to feel free to comment. You can find the class on www.candacenadinebreen.com; click the "Healing from Trauma" tab.

Again, acceptance does not mean that you are okay with whatever traumatic event happened. Acceptance means taking the situation for what it is without judgment. That doesn't mean dismissing the situation as though it never happened. You are going to have feelings that are attached to the trauma you experienced. Feel what you need to feel. Get it out of your system! If you feel like screaming, then scream (find a safe location to do so, where you won't disturb others; or just scream as loud as you can into a pillow). If you feel like crying, then cry. Accept these feelings as part of your healing journey. Allow yourself to be in the pain of that traumatic moment and experience your emotions.

When I was dealing with my issues of being abandoned by my mother, I mistakenly tried to investigate why it happened. I would sit alone and spend hours thinking about what happened to me, replaying various incidents over repeatedly in my mind to see if I had missed anything. While I was doing this, I wasn't detaching myself from the events. It was as though the events were occurring all over again, on constant replay. My inability to look at the various incidents objectively held me back from being able to free myself from the emotions I still held within me, therefore adding extra miles to my healing journey.

Some people get creative with this step. I suggested journaling; but others have composed songs and poems, and have even used art in order to help them come to terms with the occurrence of the trauma.

How many songwriters have so beautifully told of some tragic event that has happened to them? In Alanis Morisette's song "Ironic", she goes through a few traumatic events (that have not necessarily happened to her or anyone she may have known), and adds the repeated verse "Isn't it ironic?". Looking at this in a metaphysical way, things happen, and we just observe them happening without judgment.

We just have to learn how to see them for what they are, try to learn from them, and then move on.

All too often, we hold feelings within us, causing us not to grow. In fact, it really does damage to us. Think of it this way: If you keep storing up apples in a plastic bag without thinking about how much the bag can hold, eventually the bag will break. What happens when a bag breaks? All of the contents come pouring out; and it usually leads to a big mess that requires cleanup, depending on where the "break" occurred. The same thing happens with our emotions. If we keep our emotions stored up inside, eventually we will have an emotional explosion, and everything we've ever felt or thought will come out. It might not be the right time for them to come out. It may not be the right arena for us to let our emotions run wild. We may hurt those around us when we explode. An emotional explosion is not the way to begin our healing journey. Taking the time to think about the trauma and accept what happened and then giving ourselves permission to be emotional is much healthier. Once we have expelled as many emotions as we can, then it is time to move on to the next step in our journey.

Once you come to terms with the trauma and acknowledge that it happened, you must understand that you are not to blame. As previously stated, we cannot control the actions of others. We cannot even control how someone treats us or when, how and where trauma takes place. Get any guilt out of your system because it doesn't belong to you. You don't want to take something (i.e., "steal") that is not yours.

Next, acknowledge that you are releasing any low-vibrational energy that is attached to the trauma. Any anger, bitterness, hostility, etc. (i.e., low-vibrational energies) that you have placed on the trauma needs to be set free. Detach yourself from it and tell it goodbye. Break up with the emotions and move on! Carrying around excess baggage will prevent you from continuing your journey. You don't need anything weighing you down.

Finally, acknowledge that you are allowing in healing light. Say yes to the light and all the goodness that is yours! You deserve this light, and it is good for you! See yourself surrounded by white light; and feel yourself feeling loved, protected, and strengthened by this light.

CHAPTER THREE: "RELEASE"

Now here is the tough part. RELEASE all the emotions that are connected to the trauma until you can look at it objectively. I know this is hard, and it has taken me many years to master this myself. If you still feel high emotions when you think about the trauma (i.e., anger, sadness or fear), then you have not yet released its emotional impact. It will take a lot of practice and patience with yourself.

So, rather than talk you into oblivion about it, I have included some resources that you could utilize in order to help you with the process of releasing.

RESOURCES FOR YOU

Try these exercises to help clear out any blockages that may hold you back on your healing journey. The following exercises are related to chakra energy. Chakras are the centers of energy in our bodies that play an important role in influencing the well-being of our spiritual, mental and spiritual selves. It is a mind-body system of relationship that is very important for us in order to remain balanced, healthy, and fully functioning.

CHAPTER FOUR: "LOVE"

I struggled with my self-image after I had children. My husband showered me with affection, yet none of it mattered because the self-hatred that was rooted in the negativity of my past experiences were deeply engraved into my being.

Although we sometimes overuse the word, love is really the only thing that we need in order to cure our wounds. Notice I said "cure" instead of "heal". Healing often refers to injuries that we have to face. It is a physical solution for a physical injury. To cure is to actually see the result of something that was used to heal someone's illness. It is the part that is hidden. Think of giving someone medicine (physical) to heal the person who is looking and acting sick (all physical observations), caused by a virus that is in the person (the hidden self). The medicine acts as the cure for the virus, and the result of the virus being cured can be seen on the outside of the person. For the purpose of this book, we will use the word "heal" to mean curing the entire person whose wounds could be both seen and unseen.

At one point of time or another, we have all experienced various negative feelings like betrayal, anger and sadness. It is easy to understand these feelings, but difficult to acknowledge them; and even more difficult to forget them. It is usually thought that such feelings gradually go away. This can be true, but the process usually takes a lot of time and can lead to pessimism. Thus, it is important to get rid of such feelings as soon as possible. This has also been acknowledged by psychologists, and many healing practices have been introduced in relation to this. Although the healing practices have not yet been recognized as scientific in nature like psychology is, they have proved to be good for relieving tension and stress.

The various processes or techniques that we use for healing the hidden self are not new. They have been used and worked upon in many parts of the world for thousands of years. Techniques such as yoga, meditation, aromatherapy and Reiki have been used for centuries. In fact, the ancient Chinese, Japanese, Indian, Sri Lankan, Greek and Roman civilizations can be credited for inventing such easy and highly effective techniques. These techniques gain their inspiration from nature, and their resources are used in their respective processes. Continuous practice of these techniques also brings us closer to nature, and can become the greatest source of healing the feelings associated with past trauma.

The techniques of healing the hidden self are easy to learn, and just as equally easy to use. They can be practiced anywhere. It is not necessary to go through a training process in order to learn these techniques. They can be learned through magazines, books, the internet, or through classes that are being taught throughout the world. Unlike aerobics, it's not necessary to have some kind of supervision while practicing them. However, it is necessary to take some precautions when children become involved in the practices since they may need guidance. Certain techniques like Reiki can be learned only from a Reiki Master, but can be practiced independently. Many centers around the world teach this unique meditative and healing technique.

For healing the negative feelings and the wounds that they have caused, it is first necessary to acknowledge them. Since women tend to be more emotional and, for the most part, succeed in expressing their innermost feelings, this step may be somewhat easy. Women often cry to show that they are hurt. However, this is not easy for men, especially since society considers a crying man to be weak and feminine. This needs to be overcome by men because crying usually is the first step toward healing the hidden self. After this, it becomes easier to use the processes in a better manner.

When these techniques are practiced, they help us concentrate all our senses on our inner self. We are able to explore all our strengths and weaknesses, and can thus work upon improving them. By doing this, we are able to restore and strengthen positive feelings. This restored positive aspect toward ourselves is further developed into a positive outlook toward life. Problems are then seen as mere stepping stones toward more positive occurrences. The hurdles and the process of solving them become an act of improving the self and developing into a better human being.

Loving the self involves the ability to acquire the encouragement of the self, and to continue believing in the self and its abilities. We must learn to trust ourselves rather than expect something from some external source.

There's no better way to heal the self than working through the process of getting better on our own. It has been proven that people can survive better without fabricated medicines or development classes. In essence, we can heal our own being. We must learn to respect ourselves, love ourselves, and believe in ourselves in order for us to stay focused and continue on our journey.

When we are strong, we can face any challenge that comes our way. We can begin our healing journey by making our inner consciousness our best friend, and then allow ourselves to enjoy life rather than fret over the difficulties. We must keep in mind that we do not have control in all instances, so we should let go of what is out of our hands.

The "How?"

We must work through negative thinking. We can accomplish success much faster by letting go of any and all negativity. Negative thoughts, when developed, can become our worst enemy. We must never give permission for these thoughts to disrupt our potential accomplishments. Many problems develop because negative thoughts take over. When the mind is preoccupied with all these stressors and burdens, it becomes next to impossible to accomplish anything! Rather than loving others and material things, we need to learn to love ourselves.

If we learn the meaning of self-realization, we become aware of our potential. If we expect others to hand us what we need on a platter, then it is likely that we will never see the day when we become acquainted with ourselves until we start developing our independence.

We must not blame others if we happen to fall short of our goals, or temporarily get off-course. It's okay. We need to love ourselves through the difficulties and be gentle with ourselves.

In our minds, we have a window, which includes the inner consciousness. This consciousness nourishes the soul by allowing good thoughts to circulate in our minds, but we need to work with this consciousness in order to allow it the room to help ourselves. Our consciousness will move us toward love of self and toward feeling and giving love.

When we love ourselves regardless of setbacks, we will start discovering who we truly are. When we practice meditation, we will begin to see the results of healing our hidden selves. Remember, we also have the option to use our self-talk tools. Self-talk alone will inspire us by helping us to find answers to our problems.

If we use every tool that we have within ourselves, we will find our way to heal the hidden self. Other options include physical activities such as exercise. When the joints and muscles are tense from lack of mobility, we will endure enormous stress that targets the emotions. Our joints and muscles rely on oxygen and mobility in order to keep them strong and functioning properly. When they lack these necessities, our blood moves slowly through the body and mind, thus weakening blood cell production.

Therefore, if we are seeking ways to work toward healing the self, we might want to consider meditation, self-talk and exercise. It is important for us to remember that we must take some time to learn the best practices and workouts to encourage healthy living.

CHAPTER FIVE: "GET UP!"

Now, it is time for you to firmly walk your healing journey with confidence, even if you don't feel one hundred percent confident. Get up and get on the path, and keep walking! Even if you stumble on your path, get back up, get back on course, and keep moving forward!

Post reminders around your house, office space or car so that your journey is at the forefront of your mind. These reminders can be sticky notes with an inspirational quote, a checklist, or a positive affirmation, to name a few options. Even something as simple as "Keep smiling" posted on your bathroom mirror could go a long way in keeping you focused on your journey. We all have bumps on our road, but we must always get up!

You've done the crucial steps! Now you have to keep moving. As hard as it may be, get up every morning fixed upon your healing journey, and just walk. Mentally see yourself actually doing the healing journey and making the changes to stay strong.

CHAPTER SIX: "POSITIVE ENERGY, AFFIRMATIONS AND MANTRAS"

The more we tell ourselves something, the more we believe it. The same is true when others tell us something about ourselves repeatedly. When these repetitions are negative, they do not serve us well.

What we need to do is to reprogram ourselves by utilizing positive affirmations. Positive affirmations give out positive energy which greatly boosts us.

The Power of Affirmations

The 6 Ps of Effective Affirmations:

1. **Possible**: We must believe our affirmation is possible. We don't necessarily have to believe it 100% yet, but at least we have to reasonably believe that it is possible and reasonable.

2. **Power**: Our affirmation must be within our control. Affirmations are what we are telling our own brains to take action on. Affirming that it won't rain on our wedding day or that our boyfriend will stop being so critical is ineffective because they're outside our control. Instead, we can affirm that we will find great joy in our wedding, regardless of the weather; or that we

will communicate openly and honestly about how we feel, and take constructive criticism with grace.

3. **Present**: We can write affirmations in the present tense—as if it's happening now. We can use words like "am" instead of "will".

4. **Personal**: We can use "I" statements. Again, keep our affirmations focused on ourselves, and not on things outside of ourselves.

5. **Positive**: We can focus on what we DO want, not what we DO NOT want. We must avoid words such as "not" and "don't". For example, instead of saying "I am not yelling at

my kids," we can say "I am speaking to my kids constructively and lovingly."

6. **Passion**: The key ingredient to effective affirmations is to FEEL IT! The emotional response to our affirmation statement is what allows the brain to create new wires. This is also why using incantations is so powerful.

In order to reprogram our way of thinking, we will need to repeat our affirmations consistently. This means repeating them often, and over a long period of time. We need to write them down and post them somewhere visible in the home. We can even program an alarm to remind us to look at them at specific times of the day. A copy of the affirmations could be kept in the phone or wallet. It is also important that we commit to reviewing or looking at it daily for 30 days.

KICKING BUTT WITH INCANTATIONS

Incantations take affirmations a step further, and make them PHYSICAL. What affirmations (from daily affirmation activities) could be used as an incantation? A new one can always be written, and can even be as simple as "I am confident!"

What movement could be made while reciting this incantation? Some examples include: Raising hands in the air in a cheer, pulling in the elbow as if to say "Yes!", and jumping up and down or dancing.

Incantations help solidify our affirmations and draw upon our new positive energy. Armed with incantations, we have a better chance of making positive changes in our lives and making these changes stick.

MANTRAS

To most people, the word "mantra" gives off an aura of mystery and mystique. If properly understood and used, mantras can indeed produce powerful results. These have the essence of humanity; thus, everything that's verbalized has some unseen power connected to it. This power becomes evident when seriously practiced. Conceptual ideas remain just that until they are actually verbalized.

Predominantly practiced in ancient cultures, the Christian Bible makes references to the power of the spoken word as well.

MANTRA BACKGROUND

There are many explanations for the complexity of the mantra, especially when thinking that saying the word produces an actual physical vibration. If the meanings behind the words are strong enough, then the vibration takes on a level of significance, bringing energy to the words. The combination of the spoken word and the mental influence produces a "power" that causes the intent to be significant.

The general understanding is that there is power in the word, but this power is released and magnified only when it is actually verbalized.

In exploring mantras deeper, further connections to the human consciousness can be made. The human body consists of various organs which have specific functions, but have to work as one entity in order to facilitate optimum existence. Venturing into the world of mantras can be daunting and frightening, yet surprisingly inspiring. Mantras are also used as tools of and for power. Although understanding mantras can be a bit confusing, they are nevertheless very powerful.

Simply put, mantras have the means to set the mind free. As the mind becomes open and free to "explore", a mantra practitioner is able to dip into the essence of cosmic existence. Along the way, the understanding of the vibration of elements and its connections become more enlightening. Basically, mantras are a connection to the power of the spoken word or sound.

It is a popular belief and accepted truth that repeating a mantra expounds tremendous power. Those who are very knowledgeable of mantras can attest to this unexplained but ever-present power. Abundance can take many forms such as health, wealth, and friends (to name a few), all of which can be successfully attained with the influence of mantras as a result of repetitive chants. This then releases the unseen power in vibrations that work cosmically with the desired results.

Each mantra is said to be like its original source of an actual sage or historical person. Most of these traditional practices predate the written speech, and further emphasizes the power of the spoken word. There is also a direct link between the mantra sound and the chakras. The power of the mantra is explained as that of fire, which is known for its destructive and helpful qualities. The power derived from mantras can be very destructive and energy-sapping if not practiced under strict supervision by an experienced person.

POSSIBLE MANTRA PROBLEMS

When we hear something consistently enough, there is a very real possibility that it eventually becomes a reality in our minds. Repeating a rumor enough times causes it to eventually become a wrongly accepted truth. That's the power of the spoken word.

Many "gurus" today advocate speaking out a desire repetitively, with the intention of seeing it successfully manifest into reality. The only problem with this is that some people take this literally, and therefore do not put in any physical effort to reach the desired goal in the first place.

There are yet others who take the mantra practice to the extreme, which can eventually lead to occult practices. Rituals and other negative elements are added on to create the environment needed to cause intimidation and control. Of course, this wasn't the intention, but it's not uncommon.

As the mantra incantations are said to create powerful vibes that are meant to "attract" cosmic forces, this power should never be underestimated or taken for granted. Just as these "outside" powers can be used to achieve good, it can just as easily be used to achieve the opposite results.

The process of healing our spiritual, physical and psychological selves should not be considered over and above actual medical help when addressing an ailment or illness. It should be used as a complementary feature with a positive influence.

In seeking alternatives to mainstream lifestyle practices, mantras come up as a possible choice. Understanding the basic principles of mantras will assist in their actual successful practice.

Believe in Positivity

What the tongue speaks, the mind believes. By following the chanting of mantras, it is possible to invoke positive energy for ourselves and those around us. In some modern cultures, the practice of repeating mantras is a daily ritual. This ritual, if followed diligently, creates a positive mindset, which has been proven to be very advantageous in keeping stress levels under control.

By practicing mantras regularly, the positive words spoken and continually heard aloud can also "feed" the mind and change a bad thought or scenario into a good one. For those who battle low self-esteem issues, self-sabotage thoughts, and a general lack of determination, mantras are a worthwhile exercise to pursue. If done consistently enough, mantras can create a confident reality in the mind, which will then transcend into our actions and demeanor.

With so many negative elements and energy in the world today, discovering elements or practices that create good results can never be useless.

CHAPTER SEVEN: "HELP"

I have found that a good way to keep myself focused on my healing journey is to help others who may not be as far along as I am on my path, or those who have not yet begun their own journeys. Helping those who need help, even if they don't realize they need the help, creates positive energy which benefits everyone.

You could choose to become an advocate for those who are healing from a specific trauma. You could write articles or help support local shelters. You could even just be an ear for someone who needs to talk to someone who has been where they are. All of these options help to move the universe along in a positive way. When you show love, love comes back to you in an even bigger way.

RESOURCE FOR YOU

Being Confident

Building confidence is never easy, but it's crucial to remember that those around you feel your attitude and utilize it as a cue. If you're constantly complaining about your perceived deficiencies, the people around you feel your low energy and will be less than energized. If, on the other hand, you're constantly supplying positive affirmations to yourself and the people around you, even in the hardest of times, people will see your exuberance, learn from it, and utilize it as a cue to see you as truly successful.

It truly does all come down to attitude; a positive mental attitude and positive affirmations can help your confidence in numerous ways. You will see positive affirmations mentioned in most of these chapters because affirmations really do play a huge role in our journey toward healing.

Here are some examples of concrete confidence affirmations you can incorporate into your daily routine:

"I love public speaking"

"I love to share"

"My capacity to earn, love and grow makes everyone want to be with me"

"I have plenty of friends and I am never lonely"

"I can do this!"

When you repeatedly chant confidence-building affirmations, you unleash the best within yourself and turn yourself into a highly positive go-getter who is unafraid of obstacles. Making things happen becomes a whole lot easier!

When we help others, we are, in turn, helping ourselves. Helping others fulfills our service to others' purpose; and we create light energy that uplifts us and causes us to feel good, especially when we can witness the positive effects that our help has on an individual.

According to an article on the Mental Floss website, science has proven that there are several benefits to helping others:

HELPING OTHERS CAN HELP YOU LIVE LONGER.

ALTRUISM IS CONTAGIOUS.

HELPING OTHERS MAKES US HAPPY.

HELPING OTHERS MAY HELP WITH CHRONIC PAIN.

HELPING OTHERS LOWERS BLOOD PRESSURE.

HELPING OTHERS PROMOTES POSITIVE BEHAVIORS IN TEENS.

HELPING OTHERS GIVES US A SENSE OF PURPOSE AND SATISFACTION.

How can we live longer by simply helping others? When we help others, we increase our levels of happiness, well-being and health, which all help us to live longer. People who give their time in a volunteer setting were shown to have an increased ability to manage their stress and be less prone to illnesses. Those who volunteer show signs of being content with their lives because of the feeling that they are making a positive impact, however big or small, in their corner of the world. Anything that helps to raise the positive vibration of the Universe benefits us all. Also, those who volunteer are less likely to suffer from loneliness or feelings of depression.

When we do something good for someone else, that person is more likely to do something good for another person, thus creating a chain reaction of positivity. Imagine how just one community could be impacted by just one positive action! The inspiration created could change the community for the better!

I remember that when I first met my husband, hugging as a form of greeting was not a common practice in his family. Being the big hugger that I am, it was just natural for me to embrace someone in greeting. Even though some of my in-laws shied away from my hugs, I continued to try. In time, every single one of my in-laws became a hugger. It is so beautiful to see the positive change that has come over the family. Everyone is much happier. When we hug, we smile and actually feel the love around us.

It is no secret that we feel good when we have a positive impact on others. Those who receive our help show their gratefulness (even if it is just a smile or a "thank you"), which serves to validate our efforts. Helping gives us a sense of purpose and improves our sense of well-being. We are engaging with others, which causes us to be more social and boosts our mental function. The neurochemical reward we receive when we are helping others adds to our positive self-image.

CHAPTER EIGHT: "MAINTENANCE"

Healing does not just happen once, and then it's done. It is ongoing. It's going to need constant attention and reinforcement. It's like your car. You don't just drive your car and never take it in for an oil change or for a checkup. It needs constant care in order to run smoothly.

The same is true for you on your healing journey. Keep up the affirmations. Keep a journal. Remind yourself to check in with yourself and with those who support you. At times, it will be a challenge to stay positive during the day. Use Post-it notes to create signs; and put them in places where you'll see them to remind yourself that you are on your healing journey, and that you need to keep that positive energy flowing.

Take care of your health as well. If you don't feel well, then the rest of your body is going to fall apart. When we don't feel well, we are not able to take care of ourselves physically or mentally. If you are not healthy, how are you going to have the energy to embark upon your healing journey?

REFERENCES

The Chopra Center. *The Seven Chakras: A Guide to Opening and Balancing Your Energy Centers*. Retrieved from http://chopracentermeditation.com/assets/getting_unstuck/Chakraca.pdf.

Mind Body Green. "The 7 Chakras for Beginners". Retrieved from https://www.mindbodygreen.com/0-91/The-7-Chakras-for-Beginners.html.

One Tribe Apparel. "A Guide to the Seven Chakras and Their Meanings." Retrieved from https://www.onetribeapparel.com/blogs/pai/seven-chakras-meaning.

Wells Fargo Advisors. "7 Scientific Benefits of Helping Others". Mental Floss. Retrieved from http://mentalfloss.com/article/71964/7-scientific-benefits-helping-others.

OTHER BOOKS BY THE AUTHOR

After The Darkness: A survivor's TRUE story of childhood incest, rape, abuse, domestic violence, and her ability to overcome the negative impact these events had on her life (2018)

Born Different: A Woman's Spiritual Journey of Self-Acceptance (2019)

ABOUT THE AUTHOR

Dr. Candace Nadine Breen is a West-African American born and raised in Providence, Rhode Island. She currently lives in Barrington, Rhode Island, with her husband and their two children. She has dedicated her life to helping others overcome obstacles via her books, talks, and workshops.

Visit www.candacenadinebreen.com for more information.

www.ingramcontent.com/pod-product-compliance
Lightning Source LLC
Chambersburg PA
CBHW051755040426
42446CB00007B/380